The Mayan Civilization

Moments in History

by Shirley Jordan

Perfection Learning®

Illustrations: Margaret Sanfilippo: pp. 21, 22, 24, 29, 33, 34, 43, 44
Book Design: Randy Messer
Image Credits: Art Today pp. 12, 13 (top), 17 (bottom), 19, 20, 27, 38, 40, 41 (bottom), 47, 54, 55, 56, 57; Corel cover, pp. 4, 5, 7, 8, 11, 14, 15, 25, 26, 41 (background), 46, 49, 50, 53; Shirley Jordan pp. 16, 17 (top); Randy Messer pp. 13 (bottom), 30, 51, 59

About the Author

Shirley Jordan is a retired elementary school teacher and principal. For eight years, she was a lecturer in the teacher-training program at California State University, Fullerton, California.

Shirley loves to travel—with a preference for sites important to U.S. history. She has had more than 50 travel articles published in recent years. It was through her travels that she became interested in "moments in history," those ironic and little-known stories that make one exclaim, "I didn't know that!" Such stories are woven throughout her books.

Table of Contents

Timeline of Important Events

1000 B.C.–300 A.D.	Ancient hunting and gathering peoples roam **Mesoamerica**. Gradually, these people settle down and become farmers. This is the Formative Period of the Mayan civilization.
300–900 A.D.	This is the Classic Period of the Mayan civilization. More than a dozen religious and city units develop in the Petén region of present-day Central America.
900–1000 A.D. 	The cities in the Petén region decline. Soon they are almost abandoned. Many families migrate north. There they seek refuge in the newer cities of the Yucatán. The Mayan culture blends with that of the Toltecs of Mexico.
1200 A.D.	The Maya-Toltecs lose power. Their leading cities such as Chichén Itzá, Uxmal, Cobá, and Tulum decline.
1283 A.D.	Mayapán replaces Chichén Itzá as the capital of the Yucatán. It becomes the new capital for education and art.
1400 A.D.	The Post-Classic Period begins. The power of the kingdom in Mayapán declines. Many different regional states result. Their chiefs fight among themselves.

| 1502 A.D. | Christopher Columbus encounters Mayan natives on his fourth voyage to the New World. |

| 1517 A.D. | A Spanish explorer, Francisco Hernández de Córdoba, lands on the Yucatán Peninsula. Even though his horses and guns terrify the Maya, they manage to drive him away. |

| 1524 A.D. | The Spanish conquistador Pedro de Alvarado attacks the Maya in Guatemala. He conquers them for Spain. |

| 1540s A.D. | Francisco de Montejo and his son conquer the Yucatán. Soon after, Bishop Diego de Landa orders the library of Mayan books, called *codices*, burned. |

| 1540s–1821 A.D. | The Maya gradually adopt some of Spain's culture. Many join the Catholic Church. |

| 1821 A.D. | Mexico wins independence from Spain. The Yucatán becomes part of Mexico. |

| 1870s A.D. | The farmers grow a new crop, **henequen**, to make **sisal**. Sugarcane becomes another important crop. |

| Today | Ten million Maya now live in Mesoamerica. They farm and hunt much the way their ancestors did. |

GULF OF
MEXICO

Mayapán ●

Chichén Itzá ●

Cobá ●

Uxmal ● ● Mani

Tulum ●

● Champotón

YUCATÁN
PENINSULA

MEXICO

PETÉN

● Tikal

BELIZE

Chiapas

GUATEMALA

Quiriguá ●

● Copán

HONDURAS

EL SALVADOR

Mayan ruins in Guatemala

Chapter 1

The Mysterious Maya

Secrets lie deep inside the jungles of Central America. Many years ago, tall pyramids fell and became rubble. Vines crept out to smother old carved and painted limestone walls. Here and there, huge monuments tumbled onto their sides. Rain poured down on ancient carvings. The hot sun added its punishment.

The people who lived in these jungles were the Maya. Their cities were mighty. And their art was highly advanced.

But a thousand years ago, these people disappeared from the cities. No one is sure why.

Still, **archaeologists** have learned some interesting facts about the Mayan civilization.

Between 300 and 900 A.D., thousands of native workers built large cities in the rain forest. The cities were filled with stone buildings. These cities were scattered over Mesoamerica. They appeared in what are now parts of Guatemala, Belize, Honduras, and Mexico.

Mayan cities were centers of religion, art, and mathematics for many centuries. But the reason they were abandoned remains a puzzle.

Let's look back hundreds of years to a period even before recorded time. How did these mighty cities come about?

The first people to roam Mesoamerica were probably hunters. They moved about the land in small family groups. The hunters searched for animals to provide meat for their families. And they gathered wild fruits and grains to eat.

Relief sculpture, Copán, Honduras

It may be that in these places, grain had fallen to the ground. New plants sprang up. Perhaps one Mayan hunter noticed the new plants. He might have said to his wife and children, "If I put more seeds into the ground, will not new plants spring up? If they do, we won't have to move from place to place."

Planting new seeds and waiting for them to grow kept people in one place. And if hunting was good nearby, a family could build a shelter and settle down.

Over many years, this new way of doing things turned hunting-gathering people into farmers. Small villages developed near the farmland. This all happened in the Formative Period.

At first, the Maya settled along the rivers and lakes of the Petén. Today that region of jungle lies within Guatemala, Belize, and the northern part of Honduras.

There is reason to believe that these early farmers were joined by others from the south. Historians have found that sometime between the years 100 and 300 A.D., a huge volcanic explosion occurred in what is now El Salvador. Ash covered the ground. Plants and animals died. Drinking water was polluted.

As a result, at least 30,000 people left that area. Probably many of them moved north, into the tropic lands of the Maya. Their arrival caused the native cities to become more crowded.

Over the years, the main farming settlements grew into fine cities. Three of those are Tikal and Quiriguá in Guatemala, and Copán, now inside the border of Honduras. These three cities are good examples of the Mayan Classic Period.

Chapter

How Archaeologists
Learned About the Maya

The Mayan people wrote stories about themselves on the building walls and on stone pillars called *stelae*. Their picture writing is called *hieroglyphics*. And each picture word is called a *glyph*. Dates written in glyphs tell about the births, deaths, and marriages of important people.

Clay figures have been found in ancient tombs. These have also helped historians learn about Mayan people and their crafts.

Often warriors from one village fought with those from another. Sometimes the pictures on a building or stela showed battle scenes. The dates on such scenes are easily read by archaeologists. But the sentences in the writings are still a mystery.

It is hard to tell who among the Maya could read and write. It appears that priests and scribes did both. And it is likely that some of the noble class could read. However, the common people did not have or need this skill.

Each year, archaeologists are able to figure out a few more of the mysteries of the glyphs.

Detail of wall of skulls—Tzompantli, Chichen Itza

Chapter 3

Three Major Cities of the Classic Period

Tikal Pyramid, Guatemala

Tikal

Tikal was the chief ceremonial center of the Mayan people. Historians believe it took 1,000 years to build this city. It lies in the middle of many miles of steamy, green jungle in the rain forest of Guatemala. Seen from the air, Tikal seems to be surrounded by green hills, overgrown with jungle vines. But those hills are really dozens of unexplored pyramids and temples.

Tikal is the farthest north of the cities of the Classic Period. At its peak, it may have contained 3,000 structures. More than 50,000 citizens may have lived in the area. Today, only about 500 buildings have been uncovered.

The city has six huge pyramids. One of these is the Temple of the Giant Jaguar. It stands 16 stories high. It is one of the tallest structures found in the early Americas.

Tikal Pyramid, Guatemala

On top is a door leading to three thick-walled rooms. They stand in a row from front to back. Above the rooms is a large fan-shaped crest on top of the roof. This crest is made of stone and **stucco** and adds to the height of the building.

The temples are especially remarkable because the Maya had no beasts of burden—no horses or burros. They also did not know how to use wheels to help pull heavy loads. Men lifted and moved the huge stones by hand. Then they used stone **chisels** to decorate them with fine, sculptured art.

The site for Tikal was probably chosen because of the large number of **ceiba** trees. The Maya considered these huge trees to be sacred.

The lucky early settlers found golden turkeys, brightly colored parrots, and dainty hummingbirds in the trees' branches. Jaguars, deer, pumas, ocelots, and spider monkeys roamed the jungle growth below.

Ceiba tree

Finding enough water was a challenge. No rivers crossed the miles covered by Tikal. The people relied upon water holes called *aguadas*. **Aqueducts** were built from them to other parts of the city.

Flint was a valuable resource at Tikal. This hard mineral could be shaped into weapons. It was also used to make tools for the difficult job of building with stone.

It may be that the Maya of Tikal traded their flint with other settlers who passed their way. Old tombs contain seashells from the coast of the Pacific Ocean. Precious green jade and colorful pottery have been found in Tikal's tombs too. These probably were traded by tribes from the highlands of Guatemala.

Temple sculpture, Copán, Honduras

Copán

Copán was the second greatest city of the Classic Period. It was also a major center for culture and advanced study. Here the Mayan priests designed their famous calendars and further developed their hieroglyphic writing.

Copán was the southernmost city of the Maya. The land it occupied is now located in Honduras. It is likely that the people actively traded with the early people of Panama. We know the early tribes in Panama were good at working metals like gold and lead. Some of their fine artwork has been found in the temples of Copán, along with samples of tools and weapons.

Copán is known for some of the best preserved works of Maya art. These included vases, colored murals, and stone-carved decorations. Artists and sculptors were master craftsmen.

Sculpture, Copán, Honduras

These early people used **sundials** for *astronomy*, the study of the heavens. Sundials have been found at more than a dozen later Mayan sites. Priests and scholars knew how to figure the time between **eclipses** of both the sun and the moon. In 756, they built a large temple to celebrate their discoveries about the heavens.

Copán had five wide walkways. These served as great plazas.

The main courtyard at Copán featured a maze of pyramids, temples, and plazas. This whole center was ringed by tiers of stone seats. The large number of seats allowed for an audience of thousands

One group of stone buildings at Copán has been uncovered seven miles from the city's center. Since the mud huts of the peasants would have been even farther away, this suggests the city had a huge number of citizens.

Temple ruins, Quiriguá, Guatemala

Quiriguá

Quiriguá was founded in 650 A.D. It was the smallest of the three major cities of the Classic Period. Its ruins lie about 40 miles from Copán inside the borders of Guatemala.

The buildings there were smaller than those at Tikal and Copán. But it is clear that this city was well laid out.

Neighborhoods where the citizens lived formed a circle around the city center. In the center were altars and temples. Huge rocks called *zoomorphs* were carved to look like animals.

But Quiriguá is best known for the number and quality of its stelae. A wide, grassy plain stretches from the temple ruins. On it are dozens of huge slabs of sandstone, stretching

The Plain of Stelae, Quiriguá, Guatemala

higher than a human is tall. Dragging these to the plain and setting them on end must have required the effort of everyone in the city. Each slab weighs many tons.

Once the artisans had these stelae in place, they began to chisel away at them. Finally, writing and pictures covered them. The inscribed dates show that a stela was decorated every five years.

This was an advanced skill. That's because the sandstone at Quiriguá was harder than the limestone at Copán. And the workmen had no metal tools. They used simple stone chisels to do this difficult work.

Sandstone carving, Quiriguá, Guatemala

17

Chapter 4

How the Maya Governed Themselves

It may seem strange to us today, but many historians believe no one lived inside the Mayan cities. They say the huge pyramids and temples were used just for religious ceremonies.

The people lived outside the city limits. Closest to the city were the homes of priests and noblemen. Farther out were the houses of the middle-class merchants.

Beyond that circle lived the peasants. No trace of their homes has been found. But pictures carved on the stone buildings showed that peasant houses were built of mud. Such poorly made buildings would have washed away hundreds of years ago.

Each Mayan city had its own government. The most important man in a city was the *halach uinic*. In the Mayan language, this means "true man." Today, we might call him a city's mayor.

Chiefs helped the true man govern. These chiefs were called *bataboobs*. They, in turn, were in charge of less important city officials.

But even more honored than the chiefs and true man were the priests. Only the priests knew the amazing secrets of astronomy, mathematics, and the calendar. They also helped the true man govern. They were highly respected by the citizens of the cities.

Because they knew so many important things, the priests set the proper times for planting seeds in the cornfields, or *milpas*. Months later, when crops stood tall and green, the priests set the harvest time.

Sometimes these honored men were called on for medical advice.

Chief on a stone jaguar

Chapter 5

Home Life
in Mayan Times

The chief crop of the Maya was *maize*, or Indian corn. It was part of every meal. Of course, other foods were grown too. Squash, pumpkins, tomatoes, sweet potatoes, and black or red beans grew in the fields.

Let's meet a young boy of that time, the son of a farmer. We'll call him Pical.

Long before the sun shows above the trees, 14-year-old Pical is awake. Today is a special day. For the first time, his father will let him help with the planting.

Pical has pulled weeds many times. And he often works with his mother in the family's small garden next to the house. But planting a new crop in his father's fields is a special responsibility. If the job is not done right, the family will not have enough food to last until next year's harvest

Though he can't remember it, Pical knows about a special ceremony, almost 14 years earlier. He was only three months old.

Back then, his family gathered around him. With a serious face, Pical's father lifted his little son onto his lap. One by one, he showed the baby boy the tools he would need when he was a man. The tools were made of stone and wood.

Then his father took him outside. While his small son watched, the father shot an arrow. Then he quickly climbed a tree. After the baby watched all these things, he could be given his name. The name had been chosen by the priest.

Today, for the first time, Pical will poke holes in the earth. He will use one of his tools called a **dibble stick**. With it, Pical will help plant a new field of corn. His father has already cleared it by burning all the old plants.

As he folds his sleeping mat, Pical hears the sound of grinding. It comes from the other room of the small house. It's the place where the family cooks and spends time together.

Each day, Pical's mother is up before dawn to wash and clean corn she soaks at night. Then she grinds it to make corn cakes for the family's breakfast.

Over and over, she presses the round grinding stone called a *mano* against a hollowed-out stone slab called a *metate*. As she rubs the mano back and forth, the crumbled pieces of corn become finer and finer. How good the corn cakes will taste!

Until this day, Pical's father always ate breakfast alone. Women and children must wait until the grown men have finished eating. But today, Pical is going to the fields too. So he will eat breakfast with his father. Pical is no longer a child.

The corn cakes sizzle on the clay tiles in the three-sided fireplace. How good they smell, Pical thinks. He quickly dresses in his *ex* (EESH). It is a simple **loincloth**.

Now that early May has come, the men in the fields no longer need warmer clothing to cover their bodies. The men wear sandals on their feet. Each sandal has two **thongs** that pass between the wearer's toes.

Pical looks proudly at his father. How he wants to do everything the way his father and the men of the village do.

Pical's father, like all Mayan people, is short—about five feet one inch. His hair is black and straight. It is braided and wound around the top of his head. A thin braid called a *queue* hangs down his back.

As in all proper Mayan families, Pical and his father went through a ceremony of head flattening. When babies are just a few days old, boards are tied to their foreheads and the backs of their heads. The boards quickly flatten the soft bones of the forehead. As the babies grow, their faces are forced to slope back at a sharp angle.

Pical is sure the head flattening made him very handsome.

Mayan men do not shave. But when hairs do grow on their coppery-brown faces, they pull them out. Pical's father has also followed the fashion of filing his teeth to sharp points.

The sky is barely light when Pical and his father finish eating their corn cakes. His father picks up three lumps of corn dough wrapped in leaves. He hands Pical a gourd of water. When lunchtime comes, they will mix the dough and water and drink the mixture. They call this drink *pozole*.

All through March and April, Pical's father and the other farmers tore up the old stalks and vines in the fields. Then they burned away the growth. For many days, the fields smoked and smoldered. Then the men scattered the ashes and mixed them with the soil.

Now the earth is nourished and ready for planting. And the priests have said this is the right day.

As they trudge toward the field, Pical and his father begin to whistle. Whistling calls the gods nearer and asks them to bless the planting and the harvest.

Pical looks at the sack hanging from his father's shoulder. How it bulges! There will be plenty of corn for today's planting.

Pical watches his father poke a hole in the ground with his dibble stick. Pical follows closely behind, pushing and twisting to make the next planting hole. One, two, three, four, five—the boy's father drops kernels of corn into the holes. Then he shows Pical how to draw the stick across the rich, volcanic soil to fill the hole again.

The priests are saying rain will come soon. So the corn will grow. Some years there is too much rain in the highlands. And sometimes there is too little. Pical's family and the people of the village depend on the corn crop to feed themselves.

"We must honor the rain god, Chac," Pical's father tells him. "We want the god to help us with our crop."

The sun is high in the heavens. Pical's father says they have finished the planting for that day. There are other jobs to be done for the good of the village. Pical must learn to do those too.

The farmers have just finished building a noble's house. Pical knows that noblemen and priests do not work at everyday chores. Land must be cleared around the new house. So the commoners must do the job.

A group of farmers has gathered with stone axes. Pical holds his small ax and looks up at his father's powerful arms. As his father aims his ax toward a thick vine, Pical swings his small one into some leaves. Together we will finish this work, Pical tells himself.

Chac (long-nosed rain god) on Nunnery, Uxmal

All afternoon they work. Pical grows very tired. His father explains that clearing the land is one of the easy jobs. Last month, it was his turn to work on a pyramid. He had to cut and haul huge slabs of heavy rock. "The work was very hard," he tells his son. "I could barely finish my work in the fields."

At the end of the day, Pical and his father stop to see if any rabbits or other small animals have wandered into their family's trap. Trapping and eating animals is not done for sport. "A man must only hunt animals to feed his family," Pical's father tells him.

There is nothing in the trap. Gathering a few berries, they start for home.

Along the way, they pass the city's ball court. It has been some time since the nobles played their ball game. Pical remembers how people crowded the seats on either side of the field. How quickly the rubber ball flew through the air!

Ball court, Chichén Itzá

In some Mayan cities, the popular ball game was called *pok-a-tok*. In others, it was referred to as *tlachtli*. The field was 120 feet wide and 480 feet long. (That is longer than one and a half of today's soccer fields.) On each side of the field was a stone hoop with a snake design. It was mounted on a wall in such a way that the opening was upright, like the letter O.

Each team had seven players. They could only use their elbows, wrists, or hips to drive an 8-inch solid rubber ball down the court and into the air. Sending the ball through a hoop was very difficult and many games were played with no one scoring.

When they reach their home, Pical and his father are tired and dirty. Pical's mother and sister have been hauling and heating water. Now a bath is waiting for each of the men. Afterward, the two sit down to dinner. The women will eat later. But now they must serve the men cornmeal pancakes, black beans, and some wild turkey from an earlier hunt. On one or two special days of the year, they might enjoy a cup of hot chocolate.

Pical's first day in the fields has ended. Now he truly feels like a man.

Chocolate was made from cacao beans. It was used to make a favorite hot drink for special occasions. The Mayan word *chocolate* means "hot beverage." The Maya valued these cacao beans so much, they used them as money.

Chapter 6

Training a Mayan Daughter

Nuk is Pical's sister. She is almost 12 years old. Her mother must teach her how to be a good Mayan wife.

Like her brother, Nuk can't remember the special ceremony when she was three months old. But Nuk knows her mother showed her how to grind corn and make tortillas. And then she let the baby girl watch her weave cloth on a hand loom she held in her lap.

Nuk's mother gets up early to grind corn for breakfast. Some days, she lets Nuk help. Nuk is not very fast at grinding. But she is learning how to do it right.

Nuk is also learning to start a fire for cooking. She feels proud when the smoke spirals up to the hole in the roof meant to let it out.

After building the fire, Nuk checks two clay bowls drying near the fire. She and her mother will stain them with the dye from bright berries as soon as they are dry enough.

Nuk is proud of the way she looks. Like Pical, she has the sloped forehead all Maya want. And because her people believe crossed eyes are beautiful, her mother hung a brightly colored bead between her eyes when she was a few days old. Now Nuk's eyes turn inward the way her parents hoped they would.

When Nuk and her mother get up in the morning, they pull on loose-fitting white dresses called *kubs*. These are made of thin material that was woven on the hand loom.

Thatched roof home in a Mayan village

Nuk looks outside the door. Her mother taught her that sickness is brought by bad dwarfs. To keep the dwarfs away, the family puts food outside. This morning, the food is gone. So Nuk is happy. She hopes no sickness will come.

After Pical and his father leave for the fields, Nuk and her mother begin their chores. They chase the ducks and turkeys out the door. Next they sweep the dirt floor of the cooking and living room. Then they brush the dirt out of the sleeping room. While Nuk and her mother are doing that, the animals come back into the other room.

Soon the room is crowded again with pigs, chickens, turkeys, and Pical's pet rabbit. There is no way to lock them out. So after a while, the women will have to sweep again.

Golden turkeys

Before the sun rises high in the sky, Nuk and her mother go outside to draw water from the village well. As quickly as they can, they gather cotton from the stalks planted next to their house. The cotton pods have sharp thorns. Nuk and her mother are careful not to prick their fingers.

It is growing very warm. Nuk and her mother are happier when they work inside the cool house. The branches that form the roof shelter the two women from the sun's heat.

The two are busy the rest of the day. Nuk spins the cotton into a rough thread. Then her mother weaves the thread into cloth on a hand loom. It takes many days to make a new piece of clothing. Right now they are working on a *patí*. It's a light shawl Nuk's father can wear over his shoulders.

As the afternoon passes, Nuk often rubs her eyes. Since they are crossed, her eyes become very tired. Many older women in the village with crossed eyes can hardly see at all.

It is also Nuk's job to make sure there is enough firewood. When the men come back from the fields, there must be warm water for them to bathe. And their food must be ready.

Nuk knows she and her mother must serve the men first. When she dishes up the food, Nuk is careful to keep her eyes lowered. This shows respect for her father and brother.

The day ends with storytelling around the fireplace. Pical and Nuk listen carefully as their parents tell about the family's history. They have heard the stories many times. But this way they grow proud of who they are. Someday they will tell these same stories to their own children.

Chapter 7

A Very Special Ceremony

The days pass.

Pical is 14, and Nuk is now 12. They are each ready for the coming-of-age ceremony.

When the special day arrives, they are both nervous. They know the village priest is dressing in his most handsome robes. Everyone in the village has talked about the new cloth made just for him. It has shiny white bird feathers woven among the threads.

"I can hardly wait to see such special material," Pical tells his sister. "Father says only nobles and priests may wear feathers."

As the ceremony begins, the priest orders four men to help him. They make a large square and outline it with a stout rope. Then the men sit at the four corners of the square. This is now a sacred area, free of evil.

Pical and the other boys who are 14 stand together inside the sacred area. In another group in the square are Nuk and the other girls who have reached the age of 12.

For more than an hour, the priest chants while proud parents watch. Pical sees that the mothers and fathers have dressed up for the ceremony. They wear their best earrings and nose rings. And the fathers have painted their skin black. For days, Pical watched his father grind beetle shells to make the paint.

Today, the children must confess their sins. Pical and
Nuk have been thinking about this for a long time. Pical tells
the priest he's sorry he sometimes teases his sister. Nuk
admits she could try harder to help her mother.

When all the young people have confessed, the priest
sprinkles water on the forehead of each.

Then the priest smokes a special pipe. Nuk crinkles up
her face when she smells the heavy smoke. Pical gives her a
warning look. It would be dangerous to make the priest
angry.

At last, the priest chants a list of rules for living a good
life.

Now comes an important part of the ceremony. The
priest cuts a white bead from each boy's hair. The mothers
of the girls remove a tiny red shell strung around the waists
of their daughters. The boys and girls have worn these
decorations since they were four or five years old.

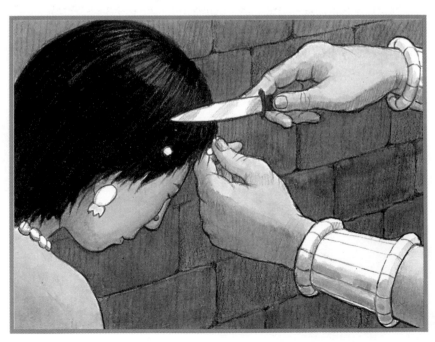

Now the ceremony is over. It is time for a great feast!

The women have prepared their favorite foods. Besides corn in many forms, there are beans, squash, and avocados. For the rest of the day, the villagers celebrate.

No longer will the boys live with their families. They will move together into a community house. And they will paint their bodies black. When they are about 20 years old, their fathers will hire a **matchmaker** to find suitable wives for them.

The girls return home with their parents. They know that a marriage will be arranged for them soon. But before a girl can marry, the families must agree upon a *dowry*. This is payment from the bride's family to the groom's. When all this has been decided, it is time to plan a fine wedding feast.

Once a couple is married, the groom paints his body. He uses a bright red color made from crushed pomegranate seeds.

Many years later, he may choose to go back to black coloring for some special occasion, such as the coming-of-age ceremony of his own son or daughter.

The newly married couple lives with the young wife's family. The husband must work five or six years for his father-in-law before he can build his own house and farm his own fields.

When he has worked off his debt, the villagers help the young couple build their house. Now they are a respected part of the village community.

Chapter

The Maya and Mathematics

People of today have learned many facts about the Maya from old ruins, artifacts, and glyphs.

We know the high priests were the educated men. The job of priest was passed down from father to son. If a priest did not have a son, he might have trained the son of either a nobleman or another priest to take his place.

The priests developed the most advanced form of writing in all of the Americas. They also created a complex number system.

Priests knew a great deal about *astronomy*, the study of the stars and planets. They were also writers, **astrologers**, and keepers of the calendars.

The Mayan Number System

When the Maya wrote numbers they used a system that is not too different from the one we use today. What has most surprised archaeologists is that the Maya understood the idea of *zero*, or nothing. They also used place value, just as we do. The Mayan system was based on 20, not 10. And the numbers were read in columns, from the bottom to the top.

One of the number pictures they drew was of a shell. This meant zero. A dot equaled one, and a bar represented five. Here is how they counted to 30

MAYAN NUMBERS

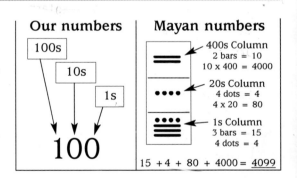

•	••	•••	••••	—	•̣	•̈•	•̈••	•̈•••	=
1	2	3	4	5	6	7	8	9	10
11	12	13	14	15	16	17	18	19	20
21	22	23	24	25	26	27	28	29	30

Mayan numbers are based on 20. They are read from bottom to top. Our numbers are based on 10. They are read horizontally.

Let's look at three Mayan numbers below.

Our numbers

100s

10s

1s

100

Mayan numbers

400s Column
2 bars = 10
10 x 400 = 4000

20s Column
4 dots = 4
4 x 20 = 80

1s Column
3 bars = 15
4 dots = 4

15 + 4 + 80 + 4000 = <u>4099</u>

Example #1

••• ⎯	One bar = 5 Three dots = 3 This number = 8

Example #2

•••• =	Two bars = 10 Four dots = 4 This number = 14

Example #3

• •••• =	The top dot is in the 20s column. 1 x 20 = 20

The next group is in the 1s column.
Three bars = 15   Four dots = 4
The bottom number = 19
So this number = 19 + 20 = 39

*Do the Mayan page numbers make sense?

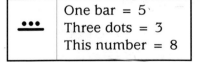

Circular tablet, Tikal

The Mayan Calendar

The Maya of the Classic Period had two remarkable calendars. One was of the *solar*, or sun's, year. It was called *haab*. It had 18 months. Each month had 20 days. This resulted in 360 days. Added to that number were five days considered to be unlucky.

With its total of 365 days, the Mayan calendar was the most advanced system of marking days used in any early civilization in Europe or the Americas.

The second important calendar was sacred. It was called *tzolkin*. It had only 260 days. These were the holy days of the year. The tzolkin calendar marked all the days for special sacred ceremonies.

The two calendars were carved on round disks. Then they were placed side by side and rotated. The sacred days were matched to the solar days. This way, the priests could identify any day by matching the two calendars and then declaring that day either good or bad.

For the Maya, there were many important divisions of time. The three known by all the people were the *kin*, the *uinal*, and the *tun*. A kin was one day, a uinal was a month of 20 days, and a tun was a year of 18 uinals. Each had its own glyph. These glyphs had few differences from one Mayan city to another.

Chapter 9

The Mayan People and Their Gods

Spiritual ceremonies were very important to the Maya of the Classic Period. Religion told them how to live their everyday lives.

The people believed that history repeated itself. The sun and moon were sacred. So were the periods of time in which they appeared.

Each day was seen as a living god who carried the burden of time on his back. In drawings, this god was shown with a *tumpline*, a broad strap passing across his forehead. This strap reached over his shoulders and held the huge load on his back.

A day god might bring good fortune. Or he might bring trouble. Only the priest could tell which. And only a priest could calm an angry day god.

Besides the gods, the Maya thought a great many things had life. And everything in their lives had souls. When a priest offered some fine pottery to the gods, he first broke it. In this way, its "soul" was released.

The Maya believed in three spirit worlds—the Upperworld, the Middleworld, and the Underworld. These three were joined in the middle by the sacred ceiba tree. Its branches reached toward the Upperworld. Its trunk was in line with the Middleworld, and the roots of the tree spread downward into the Underworld. Within these three worlds, the Maya believed there were 13 heavens and 9 smaller underworlds.

They also believed the souls of dead people moved from the lower to the higher worlds by climbing the ceiba tree. Strangely, those who had committed suicide were honored by the Maya. They went to the very top layer of the Upperworld. Those who deserved punishment went to the cold, lonely, lowest part of the Underworld.

The sun passed across the sky in the Upperworld. Priests studied the movements of the sun, moon, and planets because they believed these affected the lives of the people for both bad and good.

The Sun God traveled at two levels. In the daytime he was the bright sun the Maya could see in the sky. But at night he kept moving down through the dark of the Underworld.

In that dark place, the Sun God became the Jaguar God. Hundreds of statues have been found of jaguars, honoring this god of darkness.

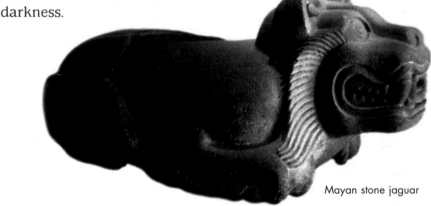

Mayan stone jaguar

Itzamná was the lord of the heavens and the day and night. His name translates to "Lizard House." He was the supreme being of the sky and the earth. In glyphs, he is shown as a double-headed iguana dragon.

Also in the Underworld were the gods of death. One of them, Yum Cimil, has also been found in paintings and statues. They show him with a monstrous, ugly face.

The Maya had hundreds of gods besides the Sun God. And because these ancient people believed that man was made from corn, the gods of sun and water were among the most important.

When a Mayan woman hoped to have a child, she prayed to Ixchel. She was the moon goddess, who was also the goddess of healing and childbirth. Women sometimes traveled great distances to pray to her.

Deities Chel and Ixchel

Chapter 10

Training a Priest

The son of a priest during the Mayan Classic Period learned many secrets.

Let's meet one of the young men who might have lived during that time.

Chan K'in is the son of a Mayan priest. His village is large enough to have more than just one holy man. Chan K'in's father is a lesser priest. He helps the chief priest govern. But he, too, has many important duties.

Now that Chan K'in is 14 years old, he is learning how to be a priest. Someday, he will take his father's place.

Each day, Chan K'in leaves the other 14-year-old boys at the community house and hurries to the temple. He spends the day at lessons in mathematics and the writing of glyphs. He studies the stars, moon, and planets.

Chan K'in is proud of the way he looks. Soon, he will be five feet tall, as tall as most of the Mayan men of the village. He has the sloped head and crossed eyes that are so honored by his people. When he finally earns the title of priest, Chan K'in will use paint made from the indigo plant to dye his skin blue. This will show his high rank.

But a lesser priest can never look as fine as a chief priest dressed for a religious ceremony. Chan K'in remembers last month when the whole village gathered for special prayers.

A new temple had been finished to please the gods. To form it, the common workingmen of the village cut and moved hundreds of huge stones. They heated limestone on huge bonfires. Then they used the melted material to coat the stone walls of the temple and bind them together. The work took five years. Then the temple was ready to be blessed.

Even now, Chan K'in can close his eyes and bring the ceremony back to mind.

The chief priest wore a brightly colored costume. It was covered with closely stitched embroidery in red, blue, purple, and green. Woven among the threads were the golden-green feathers from the quetzal bird. Only a priest might wear these as decoration. Also only the priest was allowed to wear the jaguar skin. This was draped over the chief's shoulders. Chan K'in could see tattoos all over the priest's skin wherever it was not covered by the costume.

For years, the high priest had been stretching his earlobes. They had become longer and longer. A large hole had been forced into each. Now they hung below his shoulders. Earplugs of precious stones, as large as birds' eggs, nestled in each hole.

When the chief priest opened his mouth, Chan K'in's eyes widened. The holy man's teeth were inlaid with precious green jade.

But what had amazed Chan K'in most at the ceremony was the chief priest's headdress. Atop his head, it soared to the sky. It reached up as high as the priest was tall.

In his training with his father, Chan K'in is learning to draw glyphs that will tell stories. Someday they will cover the buildings and stelae of the village.

He also learns to follow the mysterious signs of the gods that tell the right day for planting the fields.

Sometimes this is confusing. Chan K'in knows that there are good gods and evil gods. And he knows the farmers wait carefully to hear the words of the priests about planting, harvesting, and choosing the names of their children. There is so much his father must teach him about the gods and the earth.

Today, while Chan K'in's father is teaching him about the stars, a messenger runs in. A priest is needed for a very sick man. Chan K'in's father has already visited this man three times with herbs and prayers.

"Let me go too," Chan K'in begs.

When they reach the sick man's house, they are too late. He has just died. Chan K'in's father helps the village men wrap the body in a large cloth called a **shroud**.

Chan K'in helps fill the dead man's mouth with ground corn. He and his father watch the family gather its finest pieces of jade. Those go into the mouth too. The Maya believe the body will use the corn and jade as food on its journey to the Kingdom of Death.

The man who has died is not a nobleman. A nobleman would have a special burial place waiting for him. This man, a farmer, will be buried beneath his own house.

When they finish preparing the body, Chan K'in and his father walk outside the village. Another job must be done that day. It is an errand for the temple.

The two men hurry to a limestone cave. Bending low, they crawl through the cool, dark opening. With a bowl, they catch water dripping from the cave's walls. This water is sacred. Priests collect it every few days for religious ceremonies.

It is late afternoon when Chan K'in and his father carry the sacred water back to the temple. Another day of schooling ends for a future priest.

There will be new things to learn tomorrow.

Chapter 11

Sacrifices to the Gods

Chac Mool*

The Mayan people believed sacrifices to the gods were essential. In peaceful times, the people showed their respect by offering food, pottery, or animals.

When special favors were to be asked of the gods, men used the spines of stingrays as sharp picks. They pierced their tongues to make them bleed. Then they let the blood drip onto paper made of bark. When the paper was burned, the smoke rose to the gods.

In some villages, both the tongue and ears were pierced. Then the blood was smeared onto idols.

The warriors from Mayan cities often fought one another. When that happened, men who had been captured in battle were sometimes killed. Their blood was offered to the gods.

Over the years, more and more human sacrifices were offered to the gods. These rituals took place when bad things happened to the village. Wars, periods of no rain, or crop failures required blood sacrifices.

Sometimes sicknesses passed from person to person in a village. This, too, was a serious disaster. Here again, the Maya believed only human sacrifices would be good enough to ask the gods for healing.

*The Chac Mool was a receptacle for the hearts of sacrificed victims.

The Cities to the North

Between 700 and 800 A.D, cities like Copán, Tikal, and Quiriguá were at their height. At this same time, other groups of Maya had started cities to the north. This is now the Yucatán section of Mexico.

The land where these newer Mayan cities stood had a very different climate from the cities of the south. Instead of standing in a rain forest, they rose up on a dry plain. The only shade came from scrawny scrub trees instead of from jungle growth. Even the honored ceiba tree grew short and stumpy in this new land.

Mayan ruins,
Yucatán Peninsula

But the temples the Maya built on this wide, dry plain were as large and well-decorated as the ones to the south. And the village priests held power in the same way.

Trouble in the Petén Region

Around 900 A.D., a mystery developed in Copán, Tikal, Quiriguá, and the other Mayan cities of the Petén region. After hundreds of years, these southern centers of culture and the arts began to decline. Soon large numbers of the people who lived there had disappeared.

What caused this disappearance?

Historians have several theories. Some say battles between the warriors of various powerful Mayan cities resulted in hundreds of deaths. Others believe the soil, having been farmed for centuries, simply wore out. It would not produce good crops. Another theory says that a period of drought caused the farms to dry up and the food supplies to disappear.

In later years, some historians have offered a different theory. It may be that the common men, the farmers, rose up against the powerful priests. They may have grown tired of constantly working to build temples and honor more and more gods with elaborate ceremonies.

In some temples, it appears that statues were deliberately thrown to the ground and smashed. Buildings were left unfinished. And no more stelae were engraved after the year 900 A.D.

And what about the two to three million Mayan people from those cities?

Some probably moved into the Guatemalan highlands and continued farming. But they didn't have to do the extra labor demanded by the priests.

It is likely that thousands of displaced families moved north to the cities on the Yucatán plain. Historians believe this theory because the major Yucatán cities—Chichén Itzá,

Uxmal, Cobá, and Tulum—grew by great numbers during the years following 900 A.D.

In these new cities to the north, the Maya were joined by the Toltecs. They were a powerful warrior people from Mexico. Together the Toltecs and the Maya became merchants of cacao seeds, honey, cotton cloth, jade, and feathers. They developed an active trade with other people of Mesoamerica.

Feathered serpents on Mayan temple

The Toltecs persuaded the Maya to add one of their gods, Quetazlcoatl, to all religious ceremonies. Quetazlcoatl was seen as a feathered snake with open jaws. Images of this god appear on many Mayan buildings in the cities of the Yucatán.

Here is what we know about those cities.

Chichén Itzá

Chichén Itzá was the most outstanding sacred city of the north. Dotted with pyramids and temples, it was a great center for trade. The main marketplace was about 4½ acres in size. It was called the *Court of a Thousand Columns*. Here huge crowds shopped for vegetables, fruits, meat, and fish. They also bought tools, pottery, animals, birds, and sometimes slaves.

Carvings at Chichén Itzá suggest that the huge ball field was used to exhibit a life-and-death struggle. Some pictures hint that those who lost the game were beheaded by the winning players.

Human sacrifice was practiced widely at Chichén Itzá. Often those being sacrificed were thrown into a deep sacred well called a *cenote*. The people believed anyone sacrificed that way went to the highest level of the Mayan heaven.

The Maya honored Chac as the rain god and the god of the four compass points. They believed he and the other gods sprinkled rain from their gourds. When there was a flood, it was a sign that the gods had thrown down their gourds in anger.

To appease Chac, human sacrifices were thrown into the village well. These might have been enemy prisoners or young children.

The Mayan people of today still have festivals honoring Chac but, of course, there are no human sacrifices.

Chac (long-nosed rain god) on Temple of Warriors, Chichén Itzá

Cenote, Yucatán Peninsula

Archaeologists found the cenote at Chichén Itzá filled with gold and precious stones. Mixed with these were the bones of dozens of sacrificed humans. Many were children.

Even more grim is the statue of Chac Mool, a figure introduced by the Toltecs. It shows a human figure, lying on its back. A bowl rests in its stomach. Into this bowl were tossed beating hearts that were ripped from human victims. The Chac Mool at Chichén Itzá is the largest and best-preserved statue found in the Yucatán.

Uxmal

Uxmal was the most beautiful of the northern Mayan cities. It had well-decorated stone **mosaics**, rows of stately columns, and a 125-foot Pyramid of the Magician. Six main buildings covered five acres of land. Huge walls were made from 20,000 perfectly fitted pieces of stone, some weighing hundreds of pounds.

Cobá

Cobá was one of the largest Mayan cities. Its buildings were erected alongside a series of shallow lakes. The city had a fine system of raised stone walkways. Some were more than 50 miles long. These connected the central buildings to more distant cities. But, because the Maya had neither beasts of burden nor the wheel, all travel along these walkways was on foot.

Tulum

Tulum was the only Mayan settlement located on the seacoast. Tulum was a walled city. It was smaller than the other Mayan sites. Its people were fishermen as well as farmers.

From this city, canoes traveled up and down the coast of the Yucatán, and they visited nearby islands. The canoes were filled with trading goods like dried fish, turtle eggs, and conch shells.

The Power Shifts

About 1200 A.D., a leader named Hunac Ceel led a revolt against Chichén Itzá and took over most of the Yucatán. He then built a new walled city that he called *Mayapán*. It was a crowded mass of government buildings, not temples. By this time, religion had lost most of its importance to the Maya.

Hunac Ceel and his followers ruled from Mayapán for 250 years. During all this time, the art and culture of the Maya continued to decline.

Coastline at Tulum

Chapter

Men from Across the Sea

It is probably true that the first European to meet the Maya was Christopher Columbus. He came in 1502, on his fourth and final voyage to the New World.

Columbus's ship was sailing close to the shoreline of Central America, in an area that is now Honduras. Suddenly, Columbus's 13-year-old son, Ferdinand, gave a shout. He had spotted a large native trading canoe just a few yards off shore. It was paddled by Maya Indians. These short, dark-skinned men were different from any the Spaniards had seen before. Their canoe was filled with copper axes, pottery, fine clothing, and cacao beans.

Columbus and his men approached the natives. A struggle followed. The Spaniards seized the canoe and the trade goods, scattering cacao beans all about. The Maya traders quickly swam away and hid on the shore. "Look at this canoe," Ferdinand marveled. "It is made from just one tree trunk. We have no trees this size in Spain."

During the next 15 years, several Spanish ships stopped along the Mayan coast. The crews did some exploring. But no one invaded the territory inland.

The Spaniards could not have known it, but an attack upon the native cities would not have been difficult. The Maya of Mesoamerica were made up of many tribes that were often at war with one another. If a Spanish army had decided to attack, it could have defeated one Mayan city at a time. There was little chance that one city's soldiers would help defend a neighboring Mayan city.

In 1517, a Spanish nobleman, Francisco Hernández de Córdoba, spotted some men from the Yucatán city of Champoton. The Maya were standing on the shore and seemed friendly. So Córdoba and his men went ashore.

Things were quiet during that first night. But then came morning. When the Spaniards awoke, they found the whole tribe of Indians dressed for battle.

The natives attacked. They did not have fine swords like the Spaniards. And they did not ride horses. But soon most of the invaders had been wounded.

Córdoba and his men finally escaped by running to their boats and pushing off from shore. Córdoba had been wounded 33 times in the fight. Although he reached Cuba alive, he never recovered and soon died.

The next Spanish conquistador came a year later, in 1518. He was Juan de Grijalva, whose expedition spotted Tulum, the only Mayan city visible from the sea. Like Córdoba, Grijalva soon learned that the Maya were ready to defend their property. But while the natives were forcing his men back onto the beach, Grijalva had a chance for a quick look at the beautiful Mayan city.

What he saw among the idols and temples of Tulum dazzled him. It was gold! Only a few figurines were made of the gleaming ore. But those few were enough to send Grijalva home to Spain with tales of great wealth waiting in the New World. It was this news that sparked the growth of Spanish conquest in the Americas.

The next invader did not come from the sea. He came from the west. He was thin, blond, handsome Pedro de Alvarado.

Alvarado had been an officer under Hernándo Cortés. Cortés had conquered the Aztecs a few years before near what is now Mexico City.

Alvarado was leading most of Cortés's Spanish army, along with 300 Mexican Indians. He and his men swept through the central highland cities of the Maya, conquering them one by one.

Startled natives ran away when they heard the clink of Spanish armor and the thunder of hoofbeats. Both the horses and the metal weapons were new to them. How could they fight back with simple swords made of wood?

With the highlands under Spanish control, only the Mayan cities of the northern Yucatán survived. Then in 1527, the king of Spain ordered that the Yucatán become a Spanish state.

The Maya were not willing to give up their land. So conquistador Francisco de Montejo and his son, Montejo the Younger, set out to capture the Yucatán with only 400 men.

The task was not as hard as it might seem. The various Mayan cities still refused to help one another defend their land.

The warriors of each settlement tried to keep the Spaniards out. But their Indian weapons—arrows, poles, wooden swords, and hand-held spears—were not enough. The Spanish attacks continued.

At last, the chiefs surrendered. In November 1546, the Mayan defenders fought their last battle. For four months, they had held out. But in the end, they were defeated. Now the entire Yucatán was under Spanish rule. In 20 years of fighting, 500,000 Maya had died.

Thousands of Mayan men and women were forced into labor as slaves. Everyone was ruled with harsh laws. They were ordered into the Christian religion and forced to be baptized. Those found practicing their old religions were beaten and hanged.

The Spanish priests also moved the Mayan captives into more central regions. The lands they had farmed were torn up. Their fields were trampled, and their fruit trees were destroyed. They were forced out of their houses, which were then burned.

Life, as the Maya had known it, was over. To earn a living, most of them became day laborers. They had no leaders from their own people.

Valuable Records Lost

After the Spaniards defeated the Maya, many priests came from Europe to teach the Indians about Christianity. One of those priests was Bishop Diego de Landa.

Landa spent a great deal of time studying the Mayan hieroglyphics and became a leader in explaining the stories they told.

But with the good that Landa did, tragic destruction came too. In a town called Mani, the Maya had kept a library filled with *codices*, painted fan-fold books about their history, religion, science, mathematics, astronomy, and astrology. The glyphs on those pages had been carefully painted on tree bark by Mayan scholars. The work had taken hundreds of years.

Unable to fully read these valuable books, Landa decided they were full of the devil's lies. So he ordered them burned.

Three of the codices remain today. They deal with astronomy, astrology, and religious ceremonies. Unfortunately, none of the codices that were written about Mayan history survived.

Franciscan Convent in Mani, where Bishop Diego de Landa burned the Mayan codices

The Later Years

In 1821, Mexico won its freedom from Spain. This was
not a great help to the Mayan people. They were free, but
they still had no way to support themselves. Most of them
worked on huge *haciendas* owned by rich men. These
haciendas were like small towns. They had their own stores
and banks.

The native Mayan workers were treated more like slaves
than employees. They never got out of debt. What they had
to pay for food at the company store was always more than
their wages.

In the 1870s, a new crop was introduced on the
haciendas. It was henequen, a strong yellow-leafed fiber
made from the agave plant. With this fiber, it was possible to
make strong twine called *sisal*. With henequen as a product,
the farmers of the Mayan lands became more prosperous.
Some of them formed small farming villages.

Life is still hard for the descendants of the early Maya. In
Guatemala today, almost half the people are Mayan. Other
Guatemalans, whose ancestors were Spaniards, look down
on them. As rich Spanish families grow richer, the Indians
grow poorer.

One million Maya now live in the Mexican state of Chiapas. They raise corn in small fields. Many are day workers who toil for rich landowners.

But there are happy times too. In Chiapas, the Maya look forward to festivals. Women show their weaving skills. They are famous for making and embroidering blouses with pictures and symbols. Some of them say the saints give them design ideas while they sleep.

The ten million Maya of today look much like their ancestors. They are usually short and muscular. They have black hair and dark skin just like their fathers and grandfathers.

But the Maya no longer shape the faces of children with boards or hang beads to make their babies' eyes cross.

The farmers still use digging sticks for planting. But today the sticks have metal tips to break through the soil better. They grow corn, squash, and tomatoes.

The men still hunt, but now they use guns. They go after deer deep in the jungle. Sometimes they capture monkeys and wild turkeys.

After the men cut down huge cedar trees, they hollow out the trunks for dugout canoes. From these, they can catch fish for their families to eat.

Most people still speak the Mayan language and wear the traditional clothing of their ancestors.

Some Mayan families have bought land together. Their cattle graze in the jungle, and they work together to farm their vegetables. They are still poor, but they have a measure of pride.

The Maya have a right to be proud. Theirs is a long and noble history.

Glossary

aqueduct	structure that moves water from one place to another
archaeologist	scientist who studies fossils, remains of cities, and relics to learn more about past human life and activities
astrologer	person who studies the stars' and planets' positions in order to make predictions
ceiba	massive tropical tree with large pods
cenote	deep sinkhole in limestone with a pool at the bottom that is found especially in Yucatán
chisel	tool used to chip, cut, or carve a solid material, such as wood or stone
dibble stick	small hand tool to make holes in the ground for plants, seeds, or bulbs
eclipse	total or partial blocking of one celestial (of outer space) body by another
flint	mass of hard quartz
hacienda	large estate or plantation in a Spanish-speaking country
henequen	tropical plant that has leaves that yield a strong yellowish or reddish hard fiber

loincloth	cloth worn around the hips in tropical climates
matchmaker	person who brings two unmarried people together for marriage
Mesoamerica	middle, or central, America that was occupied during pre-Columbian times
mosaic	surface decoration made by arranging small pieces of variously colored material to form pictures or patterns
shroud	burial garment
sisal	strong durable white fiber used for hard fiber cord and twine
stucco	material made of cement, sand, and lime
sundial	instrument to show the time of day by the shadow on a horizontal plate
thong	strip of leather

Index